A Little Book of Little Thoughts

By Kevin Stamps

This is it
the blundering bliss
the heart jumping
blood racing bliss
This should never happen
but it's happening to me

Pondering the flavor of my
newly colored carpet.
I no longer feel the shaggy
threads flying from my
floor. Soft and squishy was
the last remembered. I
know I shouldn't worry
about such things. But I do.

Life is just one mistake
after another, and once we
get it right, we die.

No longer scented,
No longer breathing.
Once, an unstoppable force
Now a flickering flame
Prepared for death;
To be doused away.
Drinking the last
Of the oxygen
Skin wrinkling, melting
layers into themselves
Dried out from years
Of over use
now the body burns its last

There is something
stirring. These moments
don't occur often
I wish I could say
It was hope; change is the
only way to describe it

Red digits blur together as the time twists by. Lines shape oddly for unforeseen reasons, silhouettes and smiles hidden by shadows, all cascading in the center to form this. Stars collide, erupting into one, creating suns in galaxies never to be seen. It is all together lovely, grotesque and undone.

Cars explode on slow
motion sets. Spinning
shining metallic beauties
scream across the long
lensed set choreographed
to make disasters
look like magic.

Let the withered birds

break free

Time melts on

To others

I am just a moody person.

This is my body:
plastered full with lies.

This is my design:
perfection till my demise.

Why can't we ever,
so simply, align?

They
beat forcefully together

like old shackles in cold
weather

Sometimes I find myself
searching for a flaw simply
so I'll have a reason to
move on

When you are in love,
bad breadth

is contagious.

I used to dream
you were uncommon

I'm held captive
to this travesty
tearing at the heart of me
with the tension of
piano strings and a
kick drum's rhythmic
deafening

We are breathing bones
moving souls,
a piece of something
whole

Seconds spin the clock
reverse
I tinker with the
start and stop
I dream
I'm turning back the clock
just empty words and
hopeful thoughts

Riflemen and
their big machines
all set out to find a means
a source of life,
a piece of meat
to live another day

This is a new feeling

He isn't regret, remorse or
even sadness.

He is somehow, worse.

The moment you can

define the feeling is the

moment you have lost it

Sleep, she creeps to pull the drapes from our most energetic states. She decorates the homes of the soul to persuade imitation. Stencil marks and used rubber from old erasers pervade themselves across the scenery.

The voice of reason quiets her cries as the boisterous melody of waking dreams begin.

Life goes

I think she is broken.

She just keeps repeating

old lines from sappy

romance novels.

The celestial beings dance around mortality. They play strings and flutes in such a manner to attract an inner turmoil. From others, praise comes forth; inventing anthems. Thus each circle begins un aprés autre.

If two variables are independent, does is make the single common coefficient any less real? That one defining moment in which we intersect feels more real than anything else, and yet the words that have never been spoken come so easily, as if this was the right time and place to continue on our predetermined trajectory.

It's a collision.

constant and moving

infinite and finite

ebbed and unchanging

unholy and divine

Why do we desire
consistency when
repetition follows so
closely in sync?

Why do we long for
normality when the
different make the
difference?

How can we let ourselves
forget, with mortality as
short as it is?

We won't all die
but we shall all be changed

Nights are always
extravagant and
exaggerated

The laughing breeze, and
open skies leak snowfall
ever so softly.

Her voice slips
            through the air

All is well.

It lingers on.
Quietly, the memories
wade. It's different
not necessarily better,
just different.
Before, each thought
flashed hot and bright,
repeatedly enforcing the
emotions attached to flush
out and ignite fiery
emotions.

Now the lingering feelings
are a dull ache, putrid
ideas that cling to the mind
like wet clothe.
Healing is strange,
but it happens.
In time all wounds heal.

He lived a horrendous life

and then he died.

You can live your whole
life knowing everything is
wrong, and in that you are
right. It may be small
but it's something.

Perhaps the answer lies in
the unspoken language of
the heart

It begins

The fluttering of the wings.
The broken, hidden
mishaps form into a
spectacle on the center of
the stage.

Gripping to his fading youth.
Unspeakable features tend with age, shapely fingers, and large frames made of glass, cover once bright and innocent round blue eyes. Clinging clothes keep the body warm.

Just a moment,

that's it.

Then all things fade.

It is strange how easy the
keystrokes are to find. The
letters spell themselves
out like second nature.

Your entire life seemed to be leading to this choice. This decision. It wasn't even a choice, you think to yourself. This is who I am.

Stinging softly

I held loosely to edge.

I knew then

To fall was not my fear

I remember the words
on the
walls and the ceiling;
I remember the star's
foreshadowing meanings
All of me poured out
Leaving only
An empty room

Everything blurs
car doors swing
lights fly by
I can't remember
The doorknobs,
color of the sheets, or the
flavors of obscenity all
slipping away.

Cleaved
to the bedsprings
emptied rooms
just a story of chemistry
slipping away.

Desires upheaved from
such a subtle movement
A simple transition

Yesterday is dead

Today is new

I saw the sands falling into
their place, the plastic
cube lingered on the
corner, the second hand
resist before stepping into
place then it began.

Suddenly rushed, spiraling
into a fierce magnificent
blend of color and
emotion.

I am content. My heart
beats faster as my body
begins to relax. I know this
isn't really what you
thought it would be.
I am simply beginning

He left.

I don't believe I'll see
him again

I knew her. I saw her flaws, her frustrations, her admiration, her desires, and I knew the heart behind them. And the words had meaning. They signified a choice I knew I had made a long time ago, a decision I was willing to carry out to my grave.

How do you withstand the pressing in your chest, the unending reminder? Where do you find solace, peace? Is there a place, person, or action that can remedy this deep sense of loss? Will there be joy, or once again a feeling of completion?

Such a thing to behold

as pure joy

With the twitch of a finger, a stranger falls limp. His eyes darken, his feet stumble, his back straightens. The weight of such a decision encumbers him without reluctance.

What rose with quakes and quivers, yearns and aches, fear and hopes, dies down in the same manner.

The sense overloads in finality and everything turns to a muddied mess, a dim hope, and a low humming ache.

Over time the heaviness becomes normal, a simple part of addressing the morning after's and pitied attempts for newness. A day without the weighted chest becomes a distant memory.

I rely on it.

It is all that is left.

A scream brews
inside his stomach

Aching feet drag down
the weary traveler

He yearns for home
but nothing awaits him
there.

Like old crusted skin-
boiled and dry-peels with
little effort to reveal a
fresh new layer, soft and
sensitive hiding just below.

A small sting spreads as
the flesh is torn; a
welcomed and expected
pain that comes with
change

It's an extension of the
body

The bent and fragmented
mirror warps the features

Those who see the
reflection know

A farce superior to its
maker

I felt it leave my body, like an unearthly shiver, shooting outward to the farthest part of my limbs.

And then

She was gone.

I never liked to consider stories having endings. Each tale only pauses for reflection before the next stage is presented. That's how I consider this. Just one man dying and another being born.

God is always here

Among us

Inside us

(2009- 2012)

www.ingramcontent.com/pod-product-compliance
Ingram Content Group UK Ltd.
Pitfield, Milton Keynes, MK11 3LW, UK
UKHW020217250726
13967UKWH00001B/42

9 781300 454571